Little Porcupine Goes to the Psyche Ward

Little Porcupine Goes to the Psyche Ward

Frances Dale

LITTLE PORCUPINE GOES TO THE PSYCHE WARD

iUniverse books may be ordered through booksellers or by contacting:

iUniverse
1663 Liberty Drive
Bloomington, IN 47403
www.iuniverse.com
1-800-Authors (1-800-288-4677)

Because of the dynamic nature of the Internet, any web addresses or links contained in this book may have changed since publication and may no longer be valid. The views expressed in this work are solely those of the author and do not necessarily reflect the views of the publisher, and the publisher hereby disclaims any responsibility for them.

Any people depicted in stock imagery provided by Thinkstock are models, and such images are being used for illustrative purposes only.
Certain stock imagery © Thinkstock.

ISBN: 978-1-4917-7033-7 (sc)
ISBN: 978-1-4917-7034-4 (e)

Print information available on the last page.

iUniverse rev. date: 07/27/2015

A Graphic Novel Based on True Events

Chapter ONE

Little Porcupine was afraid. She was alone in the world with her three baby porcupines. She was afraid to get a job. She felt so much fear that she thought she was going crazy. So she went to see a psychiatrist.

Dr. Ostrich talked to her for five minutes and gave Little Porcupine a medicine called prozac.

Little Porcupine went home and took the prozac. In a couple days she felt wonderful. The world became a happy place. Even the wind coming through the windows was happy.

On the seventh day the happiness ended. Little Porcupine woke up with her arms frozen, her legs frozen and feeling sick like the flu. When she turned her head it felt like barbed wire ripping through her neck. Her skin felt like someone had poured gasoline over her and lit a match. She couldn't hold a spatula to turn pancakes for her little porcupines.

She couldn't sit on the floor to play marbles with them.

She stopped taking the prozac. Little Porcupine went to an Allergist named Dr. Zebra. Dr. Zebra did not know what to do.

Little Porcupine went to one doctor after another. The doctors had no idea what to do.

Then she went to a rheumatologist. Dr. Hyena looked at her and said, "You have systemic lupus erythematosus. You have to take medicine for this disease or you will die." He gave Little Porcupine a medicine called prednisone, a steroid.

Little Porcupine went home and took the prednisone. The next day Little Porcupine felt completely insane. She went outside and tried to run away from how she felt. She was terrified of dying. So Dr. Hyena gave her a tranquilizer called tranxene.

For a long time the tranquilizer pills kept the prednisone from making Little Porcupine crazy. Little Porcupine thought everything would be ok.

A year later the tranquilizer stopped working. She tried to stop taking it but she went into a black hole of despair and suicidal feelings. No one told Little Porcupine that you can't stop suddenly. Dr. Hyena did not tell her to taper off. He told her to keep taking it. Little Porcupine couldn't cook, or clean or dress herself. Little Porcupine stopped sleeping.

Little Porcupine went to the Psyche Ward of a big hospital. She thought they would help her. The psychiatrist there was Dr. Penguin. Dr. Penguin said, "You are a drug addict." He sent Little Porcupine to Meetings.

Little Porcupine couldn't figure out how to please Dr. Penguin. Dr. Penguin said, "You have a defective personality." He gave Little Porcupine a medicine called Tegretol.

Ms. Emu, a nurse, grabbed Little Porcupine by the quills and shouted, "You don't have lupus! You're faking it!"

Little Porcupine told Dr. Penguin, "I read all of John Bradshaw's books." Dr. Penguin replied, "The inner child is nonsense."

Mr. Fox, a male nurse, called out, "Meds, meds, everybody line up for your meds."

PATIENTS
RIGHTS →

Little Porcupine had enough with pills. Little Porcupine
refused to line up. Nurse Fox put the pills in Little
Porcupines mouth but she spit them out.

They locked Little Porcupine in the padded room. It was pink. It smelled like a disinfectant and shit sandwich. Nurse Emu gave Little Porcupine a shot of some kind of drug. They never let Little Porcupine out for a drink of water. They never let Little Porcupine out to go to the bathroom. Little Porcupine peed in the corner to rebel against their authority.

Every morning they gave Little Porcupine the steroid prednisone. They tapered off the tranxene. Little Porcupine became manic. Little Porcupine raced up and down the halls. Little Porcupine couldn't sit still. You can't give a bipolar porcupine any form of speed.

In the arts and crafts room Little Porcupine couldn't sit still to paint a picture.

Another male nurse, Mr. Hippopotamus, organized a Bingo game. Little Porcupine kept walking around the room. Nurse Hippo said, "You're just an adrenalin junkie."

Dr. Penguin said, "You don't care about your children. You're not trying."

"If you think this place is bad, wait 'til they send you to State," said Nurse Emu.

"They'll put you in a Retirement Home for old people," hissed Nurse Fox.

Chapter TWO

There was an endless parade of patients over the two years.

Mrs. Cow bellowed all night. She slammed her room door over and over and over. Mrs. Cow was sad because her son grew up and got married.

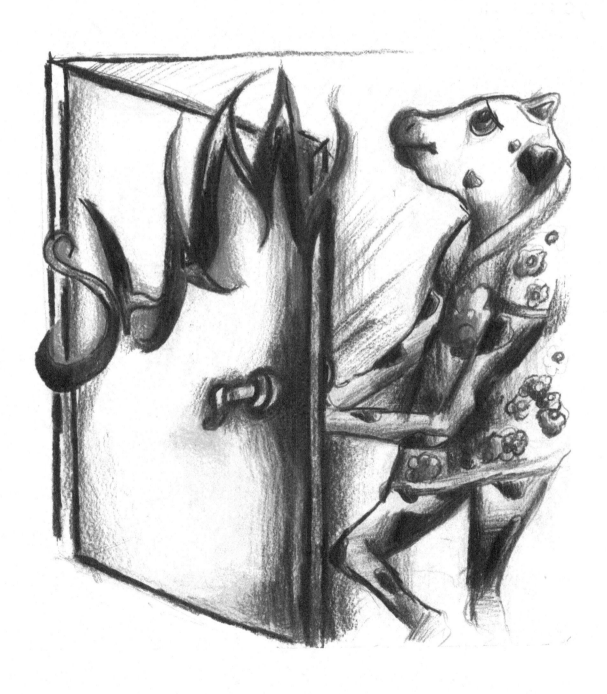

Two prairie dogs were roommates. They were locked up for smoking marijuana. They put make up on Little Porcupine. When the nurses saw the make up on Little Porcupine they exclaimed, "Now that's much better! Now you're trying!"

Miss Kitty got hit by a car. Miss Kitty was in pain all the time. Really bad pain. Worse than a stomach ache. Miss Kitty wanted to die. So they locked Miss Kitty up in the Psyche Ward. Miss Kitty hated the food there. She was vegetarian. So she lived on candy bars.

A University professor checked in like it was the Holiday Inn. He had hooked himself up to an IV morphine drip and hung out in his bedroom for three months.

Mrs. Chinchilla pulled the fire alarm. Mr. Chinchilla brought her sleeping pills that altered her personality. She hid them under her mattress. When the fire alarm went off everyone went into the center garden atrium so the building could burn all around them and everyone could be fried.

Snowy Egret was a schizophrenic who never spoke to anyone, ever. She read romance novels and stayed on the toilet for hours. She noticed Little Porcupine. In a whisper she said, "Are you suffering? Are you alright?"

Dr. Horse was an old man who use to be a doctor but now was a patient. Dr. Horse walked the halls moaning like a ghost. His long mane of gray hair was tied back. He gave himself sleeping pills all his life. But he could no longer sleep.

Now, the Little Rat was there getting her fair share of abuse. She liked to steal things from other patients' rooms. She spit on Mr. Rhinoceros, a nurse. Little Rat ran into her room shrieking in anticipation. Nurse Rhino ran into the room and slammed the door. There was screaming for five minutes.

Ms. Aardvark took showers all day steaming up her room. She was criminally insane. Ms. Aardvark told Little Porcupine that she would protect her. Little Porcupine was needy, and the nurses hate needy porcupines.

The Koala Bear had multiple personalities. The nurses said, "You'll never find a dry towel to use around her. She hogs all the towels". But Koala, all four of her, liked Little Porcupine. She fetched Little Porcupine nice, freshly laundered towels.

There was a Cuban weasel who dressed like Madonna. "I has the special powers over the mens. I can see into the future," she told Little Porcupine. She started a freakin romance with a ferret who brought his guitar to the Psyche Ward. He serenaded her. He said, "I have come to escape the groupies and find my integrity." Little Porcupine watched out the window as they left together in his sexy red sports car.

There was a gay Golden Retriever who was so depressed he came to the Psyche Ward to get electric shock treatments. At first he was nice to Little Porcupine. He sat near Little Porcupine in the cafeteria. No one wanted to sit with Little Porcupine. But after the electric shocks, he didn't remember Little Porcupine.

"I am the Lord's bride. I am unconcerned with worldly affairs. I only await His coming," a beautiful anteater told Little Porcupine.

There was a Parakeet that squatted in pretty feathers to pee violently into a Dixie cup. The Parakeet collected the cups in a row, stinking up the room. Then she sat on the bed to stare at her pretty painted claws.

A Little Sun Bear never saw the sun because he was always sleeping.

The Great Oxen was on the food line when Little Porcupine walked up. He stuck his face in Little Porcupine's face. He bellowed, "You're a Nobody!" Little Porcupine dissolved in a heap on the floor. Whatever self esteem Little Porcupine had left now was gone.

And so, the old folks who were also locked up, proceeded to dress and undress Little Porcupine in their clothes like a doll. For hours.

Chapter THREE

Nurse Giraffe strode up and down the halls all night making noise with her high heel hooves. The phones rang. And Little Porcupine never slept. Little Porcupine started pulling her quills out. It made a bloody mess. Scarification became a hobby.

The staff came in at night with glow-in-the-dark clip boards. Little Porcupine told them she was not asleep. After several months, she gave up telling them. So they wrote down that she was asleep. But she was lying there crying into a flat, dead pillow. She prayed, but God was dead too.

Little Porcupine tried to slow herself down with Buddhist meditative walking. But the mindfulness walking practice did not help. Dr. Penguin said, "You are walking like an old lady."

Little Porcupine escaped. She had to pump up the courage to sneak out a half open door. Little Porcupine hitch-hiked to a friend's house in the woods. But her friend, a bald eagle, brought her back to the mental health facility. Little Porcupine was kicking and screaming. Mr. Bald Eagle told them he didn't know her and just found her on his couch.

Ms. Orangutan was the exercise nurse. She wanted Little Porcupine to run on the exercise machine. Ruining her legs racing in the halls each day evidently wasn't enough. When Ms. Orangutan heard about Little Porcupine's escape and return, she said, "Little Porcupine, you are completely psychotic. There's not a thing you can say that would be believable. Breaking into people's houses. You are a danger to yourself and others."

Dr. Penguin gave Little Porcupine a medicine called thorazine. The pills look like brown M&M's. Over the course of two years Dr. Penguin gave Little Porcupine many different drugs. Each morning Little Porcupine met with Dr. Penguin in his office. He smelled wonderful. His suit was so perfect. He was such a gentleman. He said, "7.5 mg of prednisone can't possibly be hurting you."

"We're having a hearing on your case," Dr. Penguin told her, "a competency hearing. You will have a chance to defend yourself."

In a special room with a huge, long table, people Little Porcupine didn't know gathered. There was a Lion with a tape recorder seated at the head of the table. There was a Wildebeest. And a Llama. And an Anaconda.

The Lion spoke. "We have reached a determination of incompetency based on your medical records. Do you have anything to say on your own behalf?"

Little Porcupine said, "It's the steroid, the prednisone, it's not me. And the environment. I'm use to living in the country. It's quiet out there. I can't sleep with a noisy roommate snoring. They don't know what they're doing in here."

The hearing found Little Porcupine incompetent. Dr. Penguin said, "You have continuously debilitating mental disease". The nurses all treated Little Porcupine as if she no longer existed. She never was a mother. Never was a gardener. She was erased.

Little Porcupine told them she couldn't sleep but they told her she was sleeping and didn't know it! "I don't feel like I want to die anymore. I'm ready to go home," begged Little Porcupine. "We think you're still suicidal. You'll have to stay," said Dr. Penguin.

The Secretary Birds came one afternoon, just after the Capybara social worker left. The Capybara said Little Porcupine should try Vocational Therapy. She noted it in the chart and the chart was shuffled away and nobody ever mentioned it again. The birds asked Little Porcupine if she was feeling better. Little Porcupine reiterated, "They don't know what they're doing." One of the Secretary Birds handed Little Porcupine a card with a picture of Jesus.

Dr. Ostrich, the shrink who gave Little Porcupine the prozac, came to the Psyche Ward one day. She saw Little Porcupine but didn't speak to her. Dr. Ostrich didn't say she was sorry. Little Porcupine felt very angry. She wanted to stick the doctor with her quills.

Dr. Hyena, the rheumatologist, came to visit Little Porcupine. He still wouldn't stop the prednisone. "You are doing better in spite of yourself." But then, Little Porcupine saw a Dingo Dermatologist and he switched her off the steroid onto an anti-malarial, plaquenil. That made Dr. Hyena mad.

Little Porcupine was certain that her brain was fried. She was sure she was conditioned not to sleep. But then Little Porcupine met Little Pig. Little Pig had grown up in the mental hospital system. She spent her whole childhood institutionalized. Little Pig saw how Little Porcupine couldn't sleep. So she dragged Little Porcupine into bed with her. She put her arms around Little Porcupine. And they slept together blissfully. The torture ended.

A few days later, the nurses found out and separated Little Porcupine and Little Pig. The insomnia returned like a waking nightmare. There's a window of opportunity to escape any Psyche Ward approximately every three days. So Little Porcupine escaped from the Psyche Ward three more times.

A Cheetah came to visit with his three piece suit, dripping with gold chains and gold rings. He flatly stated, "You do not appreciate what we are trying to do for you. We will no longer accept you as a patient here."

When Little Porcupine hit the street, she found she still had the same problem she had started with. She was afraid. Afraid to be alone in the world. Afraid to get a job.

Chapter FOUR

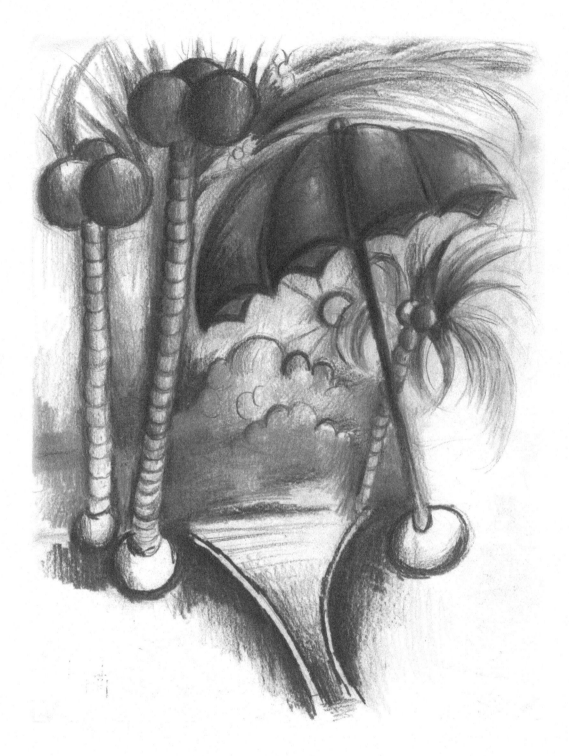

A social worker, who was a hamster, arranged for Little Porcupine to go to a Group Home. Mrs. Hamster said, "I will send you to a wonderful Group Home where you can relax the rest of your life, meditate and live by the sea."

It was in the fucking ghetto no where near the ocean and nine people were crammed into this tiny house where the owner was taking everyone's social security checks. Four men slept in one bedroom. Five women slept in the barely converted garage.

A Wolverine was left in charge of them. She cooked wonderful smelling fish soup. But she kept it for herself. She fed the tenants peanut butter and jelly on white bread with Kool Aid. Like they were kids. She kept a lock on the refrigerator.

At night one guinea pig snored. Another got up to use the bathroom quite frequently, slamming the door. Little Porcupine could not sleep in this situation either. Her youth was being wasted.

There was an old black and white TV for them to watch in the living room. Antenna TV. The Wolverine told Little Porcupine, "You're a spoiled rich porcupine." Little Porcupine went outside and pulled weeds. There was no money for potted flowers or seeds. Her heart wasn't in it anyway. Little Porcupine's children had been taken away by family.

A possum lived in this house, one of the tenants. He had caught his wife with another possum. He saw them leave in their car so he got in his car and chased after them. A high speed chase on cocaine. He wanted to kill them. Instead, he flipped his car. The damage to his brain caused him to become disabled. He also damaged his legs and walked poorly with a cane. He could not speak properly. Little Porcupine was the only one who understood his speech. He was the only one who cared that she could not sleep there. Poor Mr. Possum.

Mrs. Wolverine made fun of them. "Oh, I guess you're not that sick if you are interested in sex. Or is this a romance?"

One day the Owner came to the house. She was a Donkey. She measured the windows for new blinds. Nothing was wrong with the old blinds. She measured the floor for carpet. The floor had nice enough tile. Little Porcupine said, "The mattresses are too old." Ms. Donkey ignored Little Porcupine.

Little Porcupines mother, who had visited every day in the hospital, now came to see this group home. Little Porcupine showed her mother the metal spring sticking out right in the middle of the bed where it cannot be avoided. Little Porcupine's mother took her out of that house and put her in another. She gave Little Porcupine food stamps and some money.

The next house was larger and each tenant had their own bedroom. Everyone shared the kitchen. Little Porcupine took a taxi to the store. She came home and cooked a big chicken soup. The anorexic spider monkey living upstairs smelled the soup. She came down and ate some. The Kangaroo lady living in the second bedroom upstairs could not eat with them because she never ate with another person. Ever. Little Porcupine left the food for her for later when she could eat alone.

The owner of the house was an Iguana. He was renting to mentally ill people because his mother had been mentally ill and he felt compelled to continue the tradition. He filled one room completely with unopened packages of toys. Up to the ceiling. No room to walk about. A collection. An investment. "Don't touch my toys. Don't open any of the boxes," Mr. Iguana ordered, "Their value drops the second you open the box."

Little Porcupine no longer had lupus because it was drug induced lupus, not regular lupus, so it went away.

There was no air conditioning so Little Porcupine's mother bought her a fan. It was all very nearly normal but Little Porcupine still never slept. She watched Monte Pythons Flying Circus on the color TV and laughed.

Little Porcupine went down to Vocational Rehabilitation. The lady there was a sheep. Mrs. Ewe gave Little Porcupine some tests. Then she announced, "We can start you out sweeping floors." Little Porcupine did not go back.

One day Mr. Iguana decided to change his life and stopped renting to mentally challenged people. Little Porcupine had to find another place to live. Her mother helped and put her in a nice apartment. The apartment had a Roman tub.

And there was a fireplace.

In addition to the pots and pans she was given, Little Porcupine was handed her 35mm camera. Little Porcupine proceeded to photograph everything that was beautiful. Little Porcupine photographed flowers and trees and staircases and antique automobiles. She made everything look wonderful.

やすらぎ

Next, Little Porcupine built a darkroom. Little Porcupine spent hours and hours in her darkroom. She sang old show tunes and silly Dr. Demento songs while she developed black and white film or printed pictures in trays of chemicals.

Then she spent hours coloring the black and white prints. She used Prismacolor pencils and spread the color with turpentine and linseed oil on a q-tip. Little Porcupine had a special desk she sat at by a large picture window. She took a picture of a Buddha statue and colored it in. Her anxiety and feeling of having been destroyed subsided.

Little Porcupine was finally functional, but still, no sleep came. She put a poster of Flaming June by Frederick Lord Leighton on the wall. It was a beautiful sleeping woman. Little Porcupine called it Visual Goal-Setting.

Her mother gave her a used car. So Little Porcupine could take lots more pictures and get better. Little Porcupine went out and found interesting architecture to abstract. And a whole Japanese garden.

One day Little Porcupine saw a Jack Rabbit peeking out at her from a crowd of people. She wanted to take his picture. So she took him to the woods by the Japanese garden and took a picture next to a tree full of vines. They went to Little Porcupines apartment and took a long bath. Little Porcupine told him about the Psyche Ward. Jack Rabbit told her about Viet Nam. Jack Rabbit said, "The Psyche Ward is like a POW camp."

Little Porcupine thought the apartment had mice. Jack Rabbit checked for holes and said, "There are no mice." But every night when Little Porcupine lay down in bed, a nice new bed that her mother bought for her, there were mice crawling on her. Warm, furry tactile hallucinations. She could feel their clammy little feet. An extension of the torture of the Psyche Ward.

Jack Rabbit bought a mobile home with a pitched roof, double wide. He put Little Porcupine on one end, and his room was on the opposite side. Jack Rabbit knew the meaning of the word Quiet. He never clomped around the house like an elephant. He never slammed doors or drawers. So it was Safe for Little Porcupine to let go and sleep. Little Porcupine began to sleep in the afternoons. A three hour nap at 3 PM.

Little Porcupine had the same nightmare every day for a year. Doctors and Nurses would chase her in a building with architecture that kept shifting. Little Porcupine would fly up into the modern architecture to escape them, finding a way out in the ceiling.

Little Porcupine wept daily for her precious baby porcupines. More like sobbing. Finally, she was allowed to visit with her children. The three little porcupines had grown in two years. They went bowling and played golf and went to the beach and to the science museum and the zoo. They baked cookies and watched sci fi TV.

Jack Rabbit came into the house and said, "Here, I bought you a lap-top to write your stories. And you can play with this negative scanner and Photoshop." With Jack Rabbit in the house, Little Porcupine started sleeping from 6 am to noon. Little Porcupine loved cooking for Jack Rabbit. He worked and she kept the trailer clean. Little Porcupine is doing the best she can. She no longer is afraid to be alone in the world because she has her Jack Rabbit.

Little Porcupine took lithium for awhile but didn't like the effect on her thyroid, libido and weight. She wanted to be thin for Jack Rabbit. So she took depakote which hurt her muscles. The doctor called it fibromyalgia. Little Porcupine took malic acid for it. In the end, she had to quit the depakote and returned to 600 mg lithium and 2 mg navane. Her life was finally stable. She slept all night instead of in the day. Jack Rabbit tucked Little Porcupine in every night.

Jack Rabbit and the incompetent Little Porcupine studied codependency books and went to meetings. They did Inner Child work with John Bradshaw, Transactional Analysis to undo the patterns of Critical Parental roles, worked the 12 Steps of SLAA (Sex and Love Addicts Anonymous) and did general couples therapy to upgrade from power/control to acceptance and love. They learned new verbal skills.

Little Porcupine went to a Vocational School for Photoshop and Quark. Then Little Porcupine went to a small newspaper with her portfolio and easily got the job of photographer. The problem was, she stopped sleeping again. Every night she obsessed over each and every photo she took. Little Porcupine remembered every shot. She tried to guess which one the editor would like.

Little Porcupine took a different job as a photographer in a portrait studio. This time she slept just fine. When the shots are taken the customer looks them over immediately on the computer and decides what to buy. But Little Porcupine's legs started to hurt severely.

So Little Porcupine started tutoring in Photoshop which required less standing on her legs. And she started proof reading business letters for a large company. Little Porcupine is no longer afraid to get a job. Little Porcupine is finally receiving Vocational Therapy.